XTREME PETS
CATS

BY S.L. HAMILTON

Visit us at
www.abdopublishing.com

Published by ABDO Publishing Company, PO Box 398166, Minneapolis, MN 55439.
Copyright ©2014 by Abdo Consulting Group, Inc. International copyrights reserved in all countries. No part of this book may be reproduced in any form without written permission from the publisher. A&D Xtreme™ is a trademark and logo of ABDO Publishing Company.

Printed in the United States of America, North Mankato, Minnesota.
042013
092013

 PRINTED ON RECYCLED PAPER

Editor: John Hamilton
Graphic Design: Sue Hamilton
Cover Design: Sue Hamilton
Cover Photo: Thinkstock
Interior Photos: Alamy-pgs 11 (insert) & 22; AP-pg 7; Dreamstime-pgs 6, 8-9, 13, 15, & 29; Getty-pgs 16 & 18-19; Glow Images-pgs 10-11, 17, 20-21 & 25; iStock-pgs 26-27 & 32; Thinkstock-pgs 1, 2-3, 4-5, 12, 14, 21 (insert), 23, 28 & 30-31.

ABDO Booklinks
Web sites about Xtreme Pets are featured on our Book Links pages. These links are routinely monitored and updated to provide the most current information available.
Web site: www.abdopublishing.com

Library of Congress Control Number: 2013931669

Cataloging-in-Publication Data

Hamilton, Sue.
 Cats / Sue Hamilton.
   p. cm. -- (Xtreme pets)
 ISBN 978-1-61783-971-9
 1. Cats--Juvenile literature. 2. Pets--Juvenile literature.   I. Title.
 636.8--dc23

                              2013931669

CONTENTS

XTREME PETS: CATS

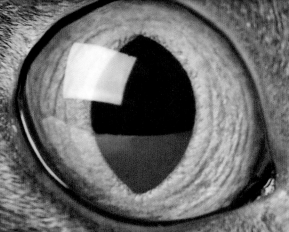

Cats have only been domesticated for about 7,000 years. Some believe it was the ancient Egyptians who turned wild cats into pets.

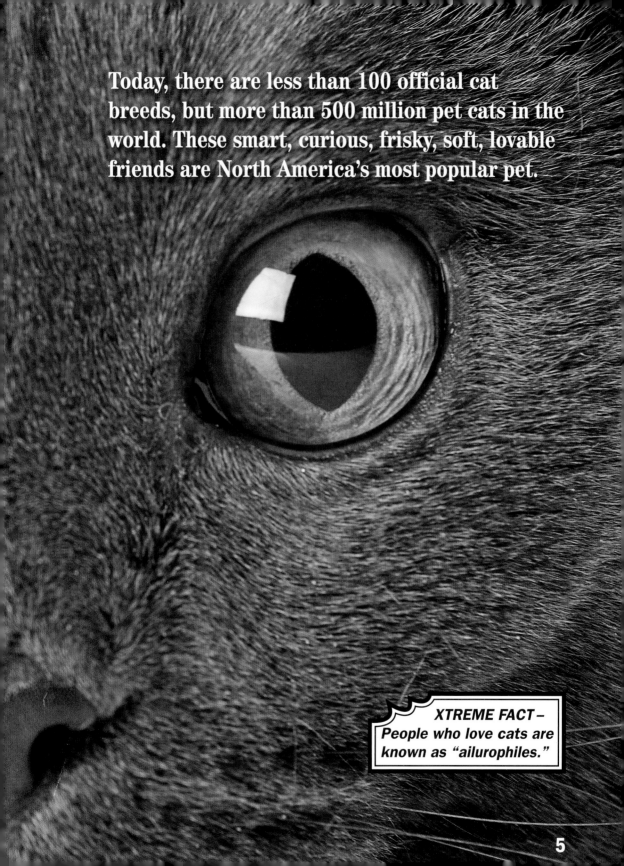

Today, there are less than 100 official cat breeds, but more than 500 million pet cats in the world. These smart, curious, frisky, soft, lovable friends are North America's most popular pet.

XTREME FACT –
People who love cats are known as "ailurophiles."

LARGEST CATS

Ragdoll cats are the largest cat breed. Big-boned males may weigh up to 35 pounds (16 kg). This is about three times the size of other cats. They are called "ragdoll" because they often go limp as a ragdoll when picked up.

Ragdoll Cat

XTREME FACT – Easygoing ragdolls act like puppies. They even greet their owners at the door.

Maine coon cats are second only to ragdoll cats as the largest breed. They can weigh up to 25 pounds (11 kg). They were originally bred in the state of Maine. The harsh winters encouraged the development of these healthy cats with thick three-layered coats and big fluffy tails.

XTREME FACT – Maine coon cats have the longest whiskers, at 6.5 inches (17 cm). They also have the longest tails.

Maine Coon Cat

SMALLEST CATS

Singapura are one of the smallest cat breeds. They weigh 4-7 pounds (2-3 kg) as adults. They are gentle, quiet cats who love their owners. They originated in Singapore. There, they are called *kuchinta,* or "the cat of love."

Singapura

Skookum cats are a new breed first introduced in the 1990s. They weigh from 3-7 pounds (1-3 kg). These curly furred cats have very short front legs. *Skookum* is a Native American word for "great."

Skookum

HAIRIEST CATS

Persians have the longest coat of any cat breed. Their luxurious fur must be brushed every day. Persians are one of the oldest cat breeds and today's most popular pedigreed cat pet.

Persian

Turkish Angoras developed long-haired coats to survive in the cold mountains of their native Turkey. Their very long, silky coats require little grooming, as they rarely mat.

Turkish Angora

XTREME FACT – Cats have 130,000 hairs per square inch (839,000 hairs per square centimeter).

HAIRLESS CATS

Sphynx cats are a hairless breed. They originated in Canada in 1966. They have a small layer of fuzz on their body. Their color is determined by the color of their skin.

Sphynx Cat

Peterbald Cat

Peterbald cats are from St. Petersburg, Russia. They have a long, slender body. As a hairless breed, they must wear sunscreen and clothing to be protected from the elements.

XTREME FACT – Sphynx and Peterbald cats have body temperatures four degrees warmer than most cats. They are sometimes used as living "heating pads" for people who are cold or sick.

BEST HUNTERS

Chartreux cats are very smart, quiet, and muscular. They were bred in France to hunt rats. They are excellent hunters.

Chartreux Cat

American shorthairs will jump, pounce, and climb to catch a mouse or rat. During colonial times, they traveled to America as pets aboard ships from Europe. These superior hunters took care of the mice and rats found belowdecks. Once in America, they were bred to be bigger and stronger, making them even better hunters.

American Shorthair

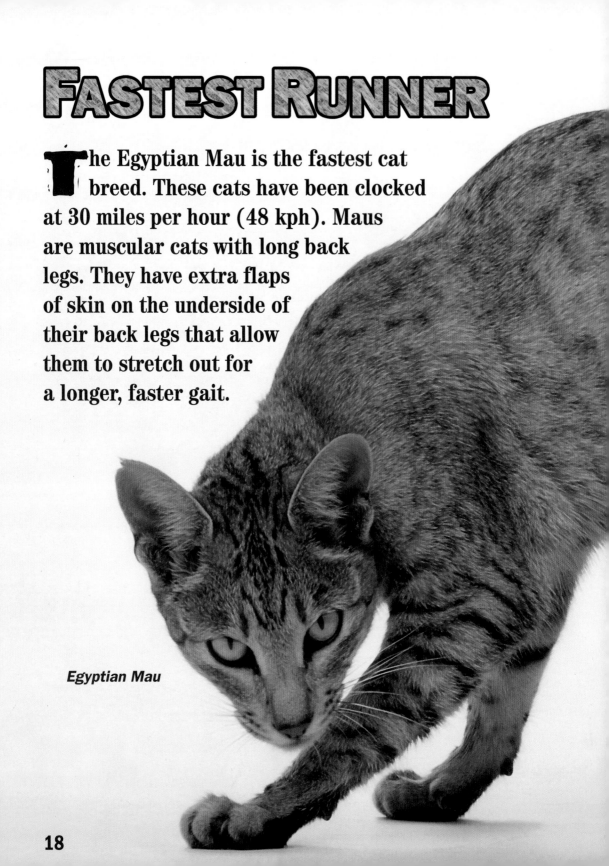

FASTEST RUNNER

The Egyptian Mau is the fastest cat breed. These cats have been clocked at 30 miles per hour (48 kph). Maus are muscular cats with long back legs. They have extra flaps of skin on the underside of their back legs that allow them to stretch out for a longer, faster gait.

Egyptian Mau

XTREME FACT – Mau *is the Egyptian word for "cat."* *Hieroglyphics of this ancient spotted cat are on the walls of the pyramids. Some beloved Maus have been found mummified. The "M" pattern on their foreheads is said to be the mark of the scarab–a sign of good luck.*

HIGHEST JUMPER

Savannah cats can jump 7 feet (2 m) in the air from a standstill. They are a combination breed, mixing Africa's wild serval cats with domestic cats. Savannahs look like leopards and have very long legs.

Savannah Cat

XTREME FACT – A rare Savannah cat may cost as much as $35,000!

Wild Serval Cat

WATER-LOVING CATS

Turkish Vans love water and have strong legs with which to swim. Originating in Turkey near Lake Van, they were said to cool down in the lake's waters.

Turkish Van

XTREME FACT – Turkish Vans may turn on water faucets, get into showers with their owners, or "play" by flushing a toilet and pretending it's an indoor fishing hole.

The Bengal cat breed came from water-loving wild Asian leopard cats mixed with domestic cats. Bengals love the water. They are known to "fish" in their owners' aquariums, play in puddles, and make their water dish a toy.

Bengal Cat

TAILLESS CATS

Manx and American bobtails are cats with the shortest tails. Manx cats are from the Isle of Man, between England and Scotland. They have naturally occurring bobbed tails.

Manx

XTREME FACT – *Manx cats have a variety of tail lengths. A completely tailless Manx is called a "rumpy." The "riser" is a tiny bump of a tail. The "stumpy" is an inch or so. The "stubby" is about half the length of a normal cat's tail. And the "longy" is a normal tail length.*

The American bobtail has a tail that is about one-third to one-half the length of a normal cat's tail. American bobtails are said to be a cross between bobcats and domestic tabby cats.

American Bobtail

SMARTEST CAT

The Abyssinian is considered to be the smartest of cat breeds. It is one of the top five most popular breeds in the United States. It is thought to have come from ancient Abyssinia, which is Ethiopia today, but may have come from India.

XTREME FACT – Abyssinians are one of the oldest breeds. Abyssinian statues and drawings have been found in ancient Egypt.

Abyssinian Cat

LONGEST-LIVED CAT

On average, pet cats live for 15-19 years. Owners who want to keep their pet cats for the longest time choose the Siamese breed. These beautiful and easily recognized cats originated in Siam, or what is today called Thailand. Siamese typically live for 20 or more years. They are very inquisitive and smart. Many learn tricks, and some even walk on a leash.

Siamese kitten

XTREME FACT – Siamese cats are very "talkative." Their voices have been compared to a baby crying. Siamese let their owners know when something is wrong – LOUDLY!

Glossary

Bobbed Tail
A tail that is naturally shorter than what is typically found on a cat. An average cat's tail is 9 inches (23 cm). A bobbed tail would be half as long, or less.

Breed
An animal, such as a cat or dog, with specific physical features that give it a distinct appearance from other similar animals.

Colonial Times
A period of time in a country's history when it is being colonized by non-native people. In America, "colonial times" refers to the 1600s to 1700s, when America's first 13 colonies were established.

Domesticated
Not wild. A tame animal that lives with people. It is believed that ancient Egyptians first domesticated wild cats to make them pets.

GAIT
The way an animal or person walks or runs, including the length of each step.

HIEROGLYPHICS
Characters in the writing system used by ancient Egyptians. Hieroglyphs are usually pictures that represent things. Hieroglyphs of cats are on the pyramids in Egypt.

LUXURIOUS
Extremely beautiful or expensive. Not at all common. On a cat, a luxurious coat would be one that is thick with heavy fur.

PEDIGREED
An animal, such as a cat, whose parents, grandparents, and continuing ancestors over many generations are all of the same breed. All of the ancestors are known by name and owner. A pedigreed cat will have a certificate indicating at least four generations of descendants.

INDEX